Thirty Days of Inspiration

w/

Author Angel Ferguson

Beautiful are the feet of those that decided to move pass their past.

One of my favorite quotes "

Its not just the combination of colors

that will create your next phase of life but the art of moving that will make it a painting worth sharing"

Move with a heart of expecting

great expectations today!

COPY RIGHT PAGE

All rights reserved,

Including the right to reproduce this book or portions

thereof in any form whatsoever.

For information, address Angel Ferguson's WordProcessing

11500 of the Americas, Tampa, FL 33617

Copyright * 2016 by Angel Ferguson a trustee of

HOPE & TRUTH MAGAZINE

All Rights Reserved

Published in the United States by

Angel Ferguson's WordProcessing, FL

WWW.ANGELFERGUSONSWORDPROCESSING.COM

Printed in the United States

Encouraging you to stay on the course of your positive journey, moving with caution as there are those that will come to toss a distraction your way.
I am learning to appreciate my distractions, as it lets me know that I am on the right path.

Maturity is teaching me to embrace it all, take it to God in prayer and allow Him to direct my path!
It's in those times of distractions that we learn just who we really are
and if we are true to our purpose…………..
Never cast your journey aside for a joy ride that will lead to nowhere……………………………….

There comes a time that we will question our journey. It's true, we will come upon those days and times that we will ask, "is it worth it", or we may feel like it is overwhelming. Here is what has helped me during those moments as I am forever in pursuit of seeking my purpose I am learning to trace my steps.

Yes, tracing the path that has me at the point of questioning my purpose! I have learned to step back and examine those thoughts of despair.

One thing that is for sure, when I am trying to do things my way, yes I am overwhelmed! But when I follow the plans set out for me, then I am at ease. Encouraging you to keep going forth take a moment to trace your steps, allow time to reveal where you got off track knowing that the important thing is to get back on course.

Give your potential a chance to grow & not die. It's not you that the next soul is waiting for;

it's that spirit of endurance in you that others are looking to identify with that ensures them that they can make it as well. We are forever students willing to share with our classmates!

At what point are we going to stop fighting with reality and learn to do one of two things, accept what is or make changes for what we want!

Keys To Success

If we ever intend to see any progress within our journey of life then there is one key factor that we all must adapt, which is consistency! Yes, lets learn to have a positive plan of consistency that will cause us to look at why we've become

stagnate, meaning no change!

Some may think this is simple but it is not.

No method is perfect so therefore develop what works best for you!

There is little too no room for the what if's, so I am applying this to every area of my life!

If I can't see any growth in my method,

then I must make some changes in me,

not in you!

Sending some encouragement your way,
Late in the midnight hour when we are plagued with how to take the next step, breathe & give it over to God.
As each new day brings about new challenges and those unexpected setbacks, the key is to keep your focus on the bigger picture which is the purpose as to why we started this journey in the first place!
Here is what I have learned; setbacks are a test of our faith & maturity.
Setbacks are also a warning that we are heading in the wrong direction, they are opportunities to make some corrections.
Don't beat yourself up over a setback nor allow anyone else to hold you back to where you fell, for no man is perfect but the one that has created us all.
Simply take this day to apply the lessons you learned yesterday!

I recently had a conversation with someone that was contemplating on giving up on their dreams of having a business. It was not because of the clients or the heavy work load;

it was because of the lack of support by loved ones. In this journey you, we must come to the reality that the vision, dream & desire is not to those around you but you! If your drive is based off of someone pushing you then you are only entertaining a hobby and fulfilling a need to be seen. Pursuing your dreams is something that goes beyond the surface & will not allow you to let go just because someone did not pat you on the back. This journey calls for long walks alone! It calls for silence in prayer! It requires patience and confidence in you! It calls for you relying on the plans that God gave you not the suggestions of those that have dared to go where you have been! Today, push & hold on to that passion within you! As all things take time to grow, don't give up before your harvest has had a chance to show of your works. I love you family, forever & a day!

Yesterday I stumbled against the stones of life and injured my pride because I refused to remove the blindfolds of my insecurities!

Today by grace I am able to move about, not by feelings alone but with the spirit of my eyes being opened because of the remembrance of the pain I felt yesterday!

Simply put, some actions are not worth repeating.

Yesterday, is but of a, foreshadow; of my today and tomorrow is but an opportunity I can only dream of with a desire to do better!

Life is only limited by the road blocks placed by fear!

Once you can get over the fear of living your dreams will have a chance to grow!

It's a wonderful feeling in life when you can reach a resolve of not haggling over the small things. When there is an understanding of how one has reached a certain point in life & things just don't seem to balance, please take the time to figure out of its right for you, if it's not then learn let go so that you may move forward.
Yet become wise enough to learn while you're there. Never leave a position without applying the lessons at hand as it will help guide us in the future.
Life is too precious to waste it on what could have been or if only I had done this……………..!
Learning to live in the now and to love people where they are.

After all I am no judge just a contributing positive factor in the lives I have the pleasure to come across.

When you have learned to take total control of your day by not allowing

others to dictate your outlook, then I say you have gained some powerful grace,

patience, a freedom unspoken of & are on a sure road to maturity in life! I am learning to become as one with

my words of inspiration!

Something so simple yet so profound! Don't let these words pass you by!

Life is sending a message to us all, that it will only give what we put into it……

Loving you forever & a day family!

Today I have decided to stop holding you accountable for the things I have let slip away………………………………………..
I am in this deep love affair consumed with passion when it comes to my journey!
Encouraging you to fall in love with your purpose as well!

At some point in our lives, we all must come to grips with, who we are why we are here and what impact we have made! Sitting here I have a confession to make, my prayers have changed, late in the midnight I'm asking God to teach me how to be me! Not the one that others desire for me to be, not even what my past had pinned me to be but the me that I was destined for. Today I realized that I am not the hurt I've caused others nor what was done unto me or the me that I thought I was but whom He would have me to become. My desire is this, that He will teach me how to become me so that I

may understand my purpose for being

here upon this earth! I can't say this enough, learn to move pass your past, you are not what you were yesterday. Your yesterday is what has molded you into who you are today as well as preparing you for your tomorrow! Accept it, learn from it, apply it & then teach it! Love is what will help you step over into the next level of your journey!

Simply sharing. As I was on my way to work, this song fell on my mind "I Almost Let Go" By Kirk Carr.
The words of this song says " I almost let go but God's mercy kept me so I wouldn't let go"
This is my reminder of where I came from.
It is my consolation when those tough days come.
This is my push when the odds against me urge me to stand still.
Yes, I appreciate my reminders as it keeps me grounded with an understanding of just who makes it all possible for me!
The song goes on to say, "I am alive today because His mercy kept me"!
We are not here of our own accord!
It's not over until He says it is over!
Stay encouraged family, notice the words "I almost" encouraging you to hold on tight & not let go.
Your change is on the way as you pursue it!

A journey is continuous. A path is traveled. Life is lived and dreams are made.
But without any actions they are all just thoughts!
I love you family! Take this day by storm by feeding your dreams with encouragement!

As I become older & maturing in my journey I can now understand the words & methods of my Father Apostle Namon Wilson Jr., he always said he did not celebrate days set aside by man.
Growing up, this was hard to understand, but now I have the appreciation of knowing that love is every day, not just Feb 14th!
I'm grateful every day and therefore am thankful for all that has occurred in my life and for those I have had the pleasure to share it with!
Every day I celebrate the gift that God gave us through the birth of His son & for the unselfish act of Christ for giving His life for us.
Simply put, give thanks every day! Love every day! For if we can only do these things on such appointed days, then it holds no value of the heart!

Simply encouraging you not to allow your vision to parish or to stand stagnate!

if you can look back over your life and say that It's always been this way, then somewhere along your journey growth has been at a standstill. At some point, you've become comfortable with settling for less than what you desire. We can desire change, pray about it, give thanks for it, speak about it but never actually put any effort towards it. The ability to really want a change for the better must start with the state of mind then to our surroundings. If you're just going to change your style of dress then I have a surprise for you, your change is just for the moment and can't stand against the tides of life! My change is not about how I can change you

but how I can overcome me……………………………..

Once we can gain this concept, we will all have an easier journey in life!

Embrace all that is within you! Yes, including the things that made you cry in hurt along with the things that made you cry with joy & laughter! It's the combination of these things that helping to mold you into the beautiful person you are destined to be! Simply encouraging you to

stand firm today knowing that you made it through the storms of yesterday!

Yes, welcome this new day without hesitation!

We are limited by the simplicity of our thoughts!

I am learning to examine the seeds that are being planted in the garden if my life as well as the ones I sew into!

Random thoughts! Why must our goals mirror the reflections of others?

Did he not number the hairs on each individuals head?

Though we all may cry out, each voice has a special distinction unto his ears & heart. Where we not all blessed with certain gifts & talents.

Yet as I look around this world of repeats & copycats,

I must ask this pondering question

" Why must our goals mirror

the reflections of others"

I focus on the clouds because they are un-numerable, immeasurable & unlimited just like my potential.

Note to self; it's not over yet! Keep pursuing your purpose no matter what it may look like, don't back up!

Don't slow down & don't let go of your vision!

This morning I looked over my life & have decided to make some changes!

I am closing the door on doubt & opening up to the endless possibilities!

The truth is that once I realized that I made it through my yesterdays,

I can make it through anything

If we ever intend to see any progress within our journey of life then there is one key factor that we must all adapt, which is consistency!

Yes, lets learn to have a positive

plan of consistency that will cause us to look at

why we've become stagnate, meaning no change! Some may think this is simple but it is not. No method is perfect so

therefore develop what works best for you.

There is a little to no room for the what ifs, so I am applying this to every area of my life!

If I can't see any growth on my method then I must make some changes in me,

not in you!

Change is not change when it is done out of anger, but done in maturity to avoid the anger!

Simply because I believe in the potential within you!

Just a reminder that your life is worth living!

Encouraging you take a look back over it all and say thank you for bringing me this far!

Let's push to the next positive level together in unity!

Something so simple yet so profound! Life is sending a message to us all, that it will only give what we put into it………………

A journey is continuous.

A path is traveled.

Life is lived and dreams are made.

But without any actions they are all just thoughts.

I love you all,

take this day by storm by feeding your dreams with encouragement.

When you think you've reached the end, encouraging you to hold on tight & not let go. Goodness is on the way to those that pursue it.

Your life is your life is your life…………………………

Live it without limits!.

Learn from it with no regrets or anger!

Share it with no hidden agenda!